this

made

me

think

of you

EMILY BIRD

ISBN: 979-8-9890563-0-9

discovering love is a beautiful journey

sharing it and remembering it in the middle of the noise and confusion of life—that's where true magic lies.

table of contents

shared moments 7

treasures & tales 29

echoes in actions 41

unspoken bonds 63

whispered words 87

love within 99

heartstrings 121

shared moments

i love resting my head on your shoulder,
finding your heart beats in time with mine.
holding hands, a completed puzzle.
we fit together perfectly, you and i.
maybe god made us that way?

silent phone calls late at night as we drift asleep.
you are far away, i know, but you feel so close,
your deep breath and soft voice take me away
to a place where i am holding you as we sleep.
it's a dream i hope will soon become a reality.

the wind dances through our hair
as we take a road trip through life.
we're not sure where we are going,
but we are happy to be together.

i sometimes forget
we used to be strangers.
once we met,
> *how could i forget you?*

jump rope in elementary school,
truth-or-dare in middle school,
holding hands in high school.
it's not how it was, but it feels like it:
> *like i have known you forever.*

we laugh at each other,
in the way a family does.
we tease and joke
as we set the table.
she made brownies,
i made a salad, and
you brought the side.
it's a mismatched meal
with mismatched love.

maybe we were meant to be,
maybe not.
it doesn't matter
as long as you are with me

i love your *laugh*. i love the whispered *i love you* that always comes after. i love your *smile*. i love the *kiss* that follows. i love your *quippy little remarks* that make me laugh. i love that we are *friends*. we are friends *before* we are lovers. we *were* friends before we fell in love, too.

it's how it's meant to be, i think.

the silence is *loud* between us. we aren't talking. we aren't even looking at or touching each other. still, the *love* is loud. the love between us fills the silence. maybe it's magic. maybe it's just my imagination. i don't know. all i know is that it feels right.

it feels right.

playing pretend in the garden.
racing down the road on our bikes.
stealing a kiss behind the shed.
texting late into the night.
laughing at whispered jokes.
speaking a secret language.
the first time we held hands.
saying i love you late one night.
long kisses turn into more.
it is beautiful, the story of us.
the story of two kids, growing up.
a story of two people falling in love.

every time i cried in your arms, every time you made me laugh, every time you knew i needed a hug when i didn't say so, every time you should have been angry at me but weren't—how do you love me so much? every time i fail, you are there to pick me up. every time i win, you are there to celebrate with me. every time i am sad, you are there to sit in the sadness with me. every time, you are there.

every. time.

a whisper of i love you. a laugh in the morning birdsong.
a kiss beneath the city lights. the hug on a hard day. the
gentle squeeze of your hand on mine, reminding me it will
be okay. eating quickly to be able to say something again
at a restaurant. arguing because we love each other but
have different ideas on how to show it. walking along a
beach, talking about our future. eating fast food in the car,
reminiscing on our days

together.

a movie drones on in the background, but i am not paying attention. i am looking at you. you are beautiful. you are the most important person in my life. i would die for you. i will live for you. i love you more than i knew it was possible to love someone. it's you, as it has always been.

see the stars? count them.
that's how many years i
want to spend with you.
see the grains of sand?
each one represents a kiss
shared at the bliss of dawn.
see the leaves on each tree?
there are too few to count
how often i will tell you
i love you.

sometimes, all i need is a hug from you,
and everything becomes right again.

sharing our last pennies for a milkshake;
you get the left headphone, i get the right.
a mixed playlist of yours and mine plays.
my shoes are worn down, your hat has a hole.
we don't care, though. we are happy as is.

i love when you are sleeping.
deep, soft breaths, in and out,
the lines on your face fade.
i pull you close and nuzzle in.
i pray for your safety tonight,
to whoever is listening in,
and i whisper "i love you"
just in case you need it.

i can't remember life without you. maybe i just don't want to. either way, it would be wrong to not have you here. to not laugh over stupid things. to not hug you when i am sad or just because. to not share the last piece of cake, even though i ate more than my fair share. to not plan our future together over cheap spaghetti. to not smile when i hear you laugh, even if it really wasn't funny. to not hold you each night, pulling you as close as i can. i don't want to remember a life like that.

you and i.
how did it even begin?
i don't care, really.
let's continue on,
together.

we whisper during movies.
we laugh over inside jokes.
we sing off-key on purpose.
we have a secret language.
we eat too much takeout.
we share everything we can.
we are best friends and lovers.
we are perfectly imperfect.
we are how i want to be forever.

treasures & tales

do you like it? i ask.
i know your answer:
yes, of course, i do
even if you don't.
all i can do is hope
you are telling the
                    truth.

when you give a gift,
part of your soul goes with.
when someone gives
part of their soul to you
>   *make sure to hold it close.*

let me give you whatever will cause that light to sparkle
in your eyes. let me buy you the whole world, if need be.
let me pick you all the flowers in a meadow if that's what
it takes. let me sing for you and record it and let you listen
to it over and over again. let me love you. let me show
you how much you matter to me. let me bless you, even if
i am not a god. let yourself be blessed. let yourself accept
the gift, whatever it is, because you are worth all the effort
or money or thought it took to get it. let yourself accept it
without any of the guilt.

you deserve all i can give and so much more.

i dream of a future with you,
one full of smiles and laughter,
dancing in our kitchen,
singing down the highway,
living life together.

often, it is the people around you that truly see your
worth. they see the work you have put in: the nights spent
working later than you ought to, the tears you cried when
you thought no one was looking. in many cases, they are
unable to repay you for what you have given them. the
best the people who love you can do is give you what they
can. maybe it is a long hug with a thank you card and a
dessert. maybe it is a party celebrating you. maybe it is
that thing you have wanted for years and years, but you
always pushed the want aside to bless others. whatever
it is, tangible or not, you earned it. say "thank you" and
accept it.

hold me as life's storms blow,
tell me everything's alright,
let me find peace tonight,
and never, ever let me go.

you remembered. i said something ages ago. i had completely forgotten about it, but you remembered. i matter enough to you that you kept it in mind all these months until you could finally find it again. i never expected it, i just mentioned it in passing, but here you are, smiling, as i stare in shock with it in my hands. *thank you for remembering.*

i want to give you
every little item or
flower or hug or
anything that will
make you smile
how you just did.

when you are considering
what to give someone you love
remember how it feels to be

seen.

don't give your gifts out of
obligation or the notion that
it blesses you. give in order to

love.

how much of my life
would i change for you?
that's a silly question.
i would change everything
to be with you.

echoes in actions

love comes in all shapes and sizes. love is in a hug from
a friend after a long day, reminding you: *you are enough.*
love is when someone brings food over after hearing you
are sick just to make your day a little bit easier. maybe
you will find love in a message from an old friend, finally
trying to reconnect with you, or a not-so-old friend sending
a simple *hey, how are you?* showing that they haven't
forgotten about you. love is in the tweeting of the birds,
the wagging tail of a dog, the purring of a stray cat, the
shushing of the leaves on the trees, the sun warming you
from the outside. *love is everywhere.*

this made me think of you

why did you do this for me?

because i can.

don't forget who you are.
you are the *light* that shines
in the *darkest hour* of night.
even if you don't shine bright,
you will still bring *light* to *dark*.
in a world full of *shadows*.
you can be the light of love.

a grandmother fights against the agony
of the arthritis in her worn-down hands
to make her grandchildren another gift
and see the smile it brings to their eyes.

a woman volunteers at an animal shelter,
fighting against her allergies and sneezing,
to try and brighten the lives she can.

a mother hides her tears as she gives
her food to her child while she still hungers
to keep the child safe and happy today.

a man stops his truck, blocking the road,
to allow a mother and her ducklings to go
safely across to the water on the other side
because all life is equal and valuable to him.

gravity pulls planets,
stars, and galaxies together.
love pulled you and i,
two strangers, together.

true love brings true service.
if there is no selfless love,
there will be no true service.
the blessings are only for
their ego to grow larger.
true love creates a desire
to help those they love,
in any way that they need,
not the convenient way.

who has served you this week? we take these people for granted each and every day. the cashier at walmart or the cook at mcdonald's. someone takes your trash each week. another person ensures your water is clean and safe to drink. maybe you had a door held open for your or a simple compliment given. someone cut and sanded the wood, mixed the concrete, and built wherever you are reading this. your couch was made by a whole team of people, from designers to manufacturers. the artwork hanging on your wall was designed by a creative mind. those curtains were sown by the hand of someone you will never meet. the food in your cabinets was made and packaged by strangers. someone wrote that book you have been enjoying. another person designed the beautiful cover you admire. *service is everywhere if you only look hard enough.*

run with me through the wild-flower meadows of life,
graze your hands along the tall grass, pluck the flowers,
feel the warmth of the summer's sun on your skin,
and smile with me as we exist in this moment, together.

we fell together,
crashing and burning
like shooting stars.

i saw the world in a brighter light
when i realized i might actually
be able to change the course of
lives each and every day of mine.
i watched as a compliment brought
light happiness into the tired face
of a stressed college student.
i have seen lightness work its way
into the tense shoulders of a mother
when she is told how well she is
actually doing at raising them.
i've never had to lie to brighten
the sky of someone's long day.
reasons to smile are all around,
but sometimes someone else
needs to be the one to point it out.

in business, they ask:
>   *what can you do for me?*

in love, we ask:
>   *what can i do for you?*

a mother's love,
selfless service,
endless compassion,
unconditional love.

we all need this love,
and it extends beyond
motherhood and borders.

a mother's love
ties the world together,
allows all to feel loved,
keeps strangers safe,
and fills the world
with acts of love.

your warm skin
presses against mine,
fighting off the cold
of the changing
seasons.

let's go on an adventure,
you and me, together.
bring friends we haven't
found the time to see.
let's run far away
into our own world.
love and harmony
naturally surround us
when we serve
each other so freely.

love is baked into cookies,
hammered into homes,
painted into artwork,
written into letter.
love is shown in the smiles
our acts bring to faces.

watch the weight fall
off their shoulders
as you help them.
see the smile rise
to their eyes again,
and peace find them.
let it fill you with joy,
and go do it again.

kiss me
like it is the
last time
every time

mother earth's love
is in the wind's caress,
in the sun's warmth,
the softness of fur,
and the coolness of dirt.
it's in the water as it
embraces and nourishes.
her love is everywhere.

i noticed something:
happy people, the ones
who love themselves,
and who love life,
are always helping others,
somehow making their
own smile brighter, too.

slow down.
you have more hours
than you think you do.
spend some helping
those around you.

it will help you, too.

unspoken bonds

hold me.
i know it's late.
i know you're tired.
but please just
hold me.

i like to think that i am a grown-up.
i pay bills, have a car, work a job;
i do all those grown-up-y things.
but some days, being grown is
just a little too hard for me to do,
so i go over to my mom and ask

can i have a hug?

have you had a friend, a new one, one you barely know
but are beginning to fall in love with, give you a hug, or a
high-five, or a gentle hand on the shoulder? it always tells
you how well you love them. there is a feeling, a happy,
light feeling, that fills you.

falling in love doesn't have to be romantic. your friend has the cutest laugh, and it is severely contagious. the guy you see feeding the birds in the park always makes you smile a little. there is a teen that runs past your house every day, and you find yourself proud of them for their effort. a mom talks to their crying child patiently and gently, and you love her for being kind. there's an old man at the library researching astronomy because his grandson, only four, has a new obsession with it, and you can't help but feel that warmth in your chest. the beauty of strangers is the fleeting, but ever-present, love we feel for them.

a deeper sadness finds me when i turn to a friend for a
shoulder to cry on. normal sadness usually leads to a loved
one, but what if those loved ones are the reason for my
tears? the hug of a friend, while you cry out your pains
from the life you endure, can bring greater peace than
any other. a true friend sits patiently, rubbing or patting or
swaying to soothe, and listens to your sorrows with grace
and love. find friends like that, and do not let go of them.

how long has it been since you have seen that friend?
you know which one i am talking about.
you two seem to never have the time for each other,
but somehow it seems to work out fine.
you are always able to reconnect and reunite at whim.
it is your turn to reach out (even if it isn't).
offer a coffee, a conversation, and a well-needed hug
before returning to your separate lives.

i've held you in my dreams
each night spent without you.
i've held you in my arms
each day spent with you.

you need a hug.
yes, you really do.
just ask for one.
they need one, too.

why do we avoid touch? sometimes we forget to hug our family members when we see them. we feel like we can only ask for a hug if we are in *desperate* need of it, not just because we want one. why do we force ourselves to suffer without touch? we are all suffering from lack of touch, so *why is it so hard to do?*

this made me think of you

i need a hug

how could i explain our love to someone else?
how could i explain rain to someone who has never seen it?
how could i explain warmth to someone who has never felt it?
how could i explain our love?

don't forget to hug me
before you leave today.
we never know when
fate may intervene,
and we never see
each other again.

all i need
is you
here
with me.

it's okay.
let me hold you.
let me sway back and forth.
let me soothe you.
it will be okay.

i love you.
not in the way i love the partners in my life,
but in the way i love that one song, you know?
i can play it over and over again, forever,
yet still hear something new each time.
maybe it is the love i have for artwork,
musing over it for hours in awe.
i love you like that.

i need the type of hug that lasts for hours. one that cleanses my soul, relaxes my shoulders, relieves the tension in my neck, and soothes my headache. the one that takes away my worries. one that makes everything right again. i need that type of hug.

family feels warm.
we meet under summer sun,
or in sweaters around a fire.
our time is full of hugs and
rosy cheeks as we smile
and talk and laugh and love.
family is warm.

from the right person, there is no such thing
as too many hugs.

on the days when nothing
seems to matter anymore,
i often find the meaning
when in your arms.

i will give you a hug
as many times as you need.
i will never run out.

i will hold you tonight
and remind you it'll be alright.
you can cry if you need to,
i will just tell you how much
i love you.

whispered words

i know today was hard. you felt alone. you felt weak.
it is okay to feel that way sometimes. it can be hard
to remember you are not alone. when you are in the
shadowed valley of your mountains, you can't see the light
on the other side. i am here with you on this journey. you
are safe. you are doing better than you believe you are.

look at me.
you are my everything.
you are my sun.
i love you.

it will be okay.
i don't know when.
but it will be.
i promise.

i can tell you,
over and over
all you can do.

i can whisper
in the darkest hours
that light is still there.

i can sing
a sweet melody
of how well you are doing.

none of my words will matter,
not in the slightest,
if you won't be a believer.

hold me tonight
under the city lights,
and dream with me
of the stars above.

tell me.

tell me how much you love me. tell me how you appreciate everything i do. tell me you want to spend your life with me. tell me how you dream of me. tell me how beautiful, funny, and wonderful i am. tell me about how the sun hits my face just right. tell me how my laugh gives you butterflies and how my smile fills you with warmth. tell me *everything.*

tell me again.

i'm *failing*
i have no friends.
i'm not worthy of love.
i can't do anything right.
everything i try just falls apart.
i can't keep on top of it all.
i'm amounting to so little.
i can't do this.

you are *learning*.
you are surrounded by caring people.
you can have all the love i have to give.
you become better through trial and error.
turn the broken pieces into golden-lined art.
you can ask for help with anything.
you are already so much.
yes, you can.

sing to me.

sing like a bird does to its lover.

sing in the way that words flow so perfectly.

speak the words you've longed to say.

speak like a poet writes.

speak to me.

when i've been working so hard,
and the days and nights begin to blur.
when i can't stand how far apart we are.
all it takes are a few loving words
to make it all right again.

love within

stop staring at the mirror, pointing out those so-called *imperfections*. stop *counting* the calories or *watching* the carbs. stop sucking your stomach in. stop *wondering* what they think of you. stop *pretending* to be someone else in order for them to like you. stop *hating* the way you talk. stop trying to change *everything* about you. stop *hating* yourself. *stop*.

start pointing out every perfect, *beautiful* detail about you.
start *eating* what you love. start eating *enough* of it. start
wearing crop tops and showing off your tummy because
why not? start living *carefree*. start being *you*. start talking
in a way that *feels* right. start embracing who you are *now*.
start *loving* yourself. *start*.

i don't remember when i stopped caring.
i eat what i want. i say what i think.
i wear what is beautiful to me.
i embrace my imperfections,
and i love my flaws.
but now i am
　　　free

it seems like yesterday
when you and i were young;
two lovers dreaming together
of a life that might be.

it is a miracle, you know.
out of billions of people,
the two of us managed
to find each other.

i love you as the sun loves the moon,
sharing its light with her each night,
and waiting for her return each day.

i fell in love with you
under the summer sun,
and now i stay close to you
while in winter's wrath.

grow with me,
as we traverse
the years
together.

i look in the mirror and see a masterpiece.
i look at you, and i see beauty unbound.
you look at me, and notice all the good.
you look in the mirror, and only see bad.

was it destiny,
a fate foretold,
or was it chance,
you and i?

yesterday is gone,
tomorrow isn't here,
so live with me
today.

your breath on my shoulder,
your arms around my waist;
a seemingly simple embrace

laughter
in the blankets,
kisses
on the seashore.

our paths,
once separate,
are now one
and the same

don't ever forget that

> *poets*
>
> *sculptors*
>
> *painters*
>
> *photographers*
>
> *writers*
>
> *singers*

have all admired the

> *beauty*

of those who look like

> *you*

how many stars are there?
how many worlds orbit them?
how many galaxies fill the sky?
how did we ever find each other?

don't look for love in someone else.
you won't find it, not the love you need.
look for the love you need in you.
you are the only true constant in your life.
you are the only one that knows
each and every flaw you have and
each and every perfect detail of you.
no one else can love you as fully as

you.

every day we take care of things around us.
    the kitchen needs cleaned.
    the dishes need washed.
    the laundry needs folded.
    the floor needs swept.
but don't forget to take care of you.
    your body needs cleaned.
    your hair needs brushed.
    your muscles need stretched.
    your soul needs space.
    you need loved, too.

someone sees an animal and smiles because of you.
someone does a funny dance you taught them.
someone laughs because of a memory of you.
someone wants to tell you what they heard.
someone hears a song and thinks of you.
someone wonders if you are okay today.
someone plans a surprise for you.
someone prays for you.
someone loves you.
you matter.

heartstrings

i don't know if heaven is real,
but i do know
it will be hell
if i don't find you by my side.

maybe i will be reincarnated,
given a chance
to find you
and to love you all over again.

there could be nothing in the 'after'
but i know the
stars will remember
and will tell our story.

your *embrace*

    is the sun on my skin

    while i bask on the beach's burning sand.

your *voice*

    is birds, singing my rise

    from the softness of my bed each morning.

your *skin*

    is the clouds i dance on

    each night in my dreams spent with you.

your *eyes*

    are the galaxies contained

    within wise orbs of wonder.

your *everything*

    is my world

    and my muse.

when i see an old couple
       at the grocery store,
       sat on their porch,
       walking at dawn,
       laughing at dinner,
i think of us and pray
to whoever is there
that one day we will be
       just like them.

you don't have to do anything;
>   your presence *alone* brings me joy.
my best friend, lover, and companion;
>   the *sun* on my rainy days,
>   the *anchor* in my storms.
you don't know how *strong*
>   you make me.

i thought you were another
knight in shining armor
coming to slay the dragon,
but i was wrong. you came
to finally show the dragon

love.

i wasn't sure love was real.
my grandparents bickered.
my parents were bitter.
it didn't seem it could be.

until you showed me that love is real.

i can get tired of the same meal,
the same routine, the same people,
the same town, the same route,
the same movie, the same book,
the same home, the same smells,
but, somehow, i am never tired of

you.

your presence can save me
from unseen assailants.
your embrace can warm
the coldest of my nights.
your kiss can calm me
on the stormiest sea.

something always feels missing
when you are not here with me.
the puzzle pieces fall into place
when you return home to me.

when i feel like we are falling apart,
i hold you tight and let your warmth
melt the two of us together again.

no blanket is as warm,
no bed is as comforting,
no pillow is as restful,
as being with you.

i used to hide under my blanket during thunderstorms.

> *my fears were the crash of the lightning and the roar of the thunder.*

i don't hide under my blanket anymore.

> *my fears have grown; they are far scarier than lightning.*

now i hide from them in your arms.

i didn't want to love you. i was focused on so many more important things. i didn't have the time. i didn't want to get distracted. a distraction is what you were. how naive of me.

my love for you consumes me.

i give you all my love, and all my focus now. you are my important, the only thing that matters. i would give you every minute i have left if i had to. i will spend my life distracted by you, and i will be happy.

after all, what is life without you?

will you love me? will you give me all of your attention? am i the most important thing in your life? how will you spend your time? will it be with me? do you even notice me? do i even make you happy?

answer me, please. i am scared.

it is cheesy, i know. this isn't a romance movie, i know.
but that doesn't stop the birds from singing each morning,
or the sun from rising, or the rain from falling. everything
keeps going, on and on in perfection. it rains when i am
sad, and the sun shines when i am happy. the birds wake
me just at the right time. it is perfect, even if i only think
so because of you.

tell me

that i am the most beautiful person you have ever seen.
tell me you would fight through all of hell to save me.
tell me you will love me forever. tell me how we will be
remembered in the stars. tell me how that song makes
you think of me. tell me how you miss me when i am not
here. tell me how you never want me to leave. tell me
everything you love about the world. tell me why. tell me
everything there is to tell about you. tell me your secrets.
tell me your nightmares. tell me everything. tell me you
love me.

tell me again.

our first handhold felt weird.
our first kiss was exciting.
all of our firsts are normal:
a part of our daily life, now.
my hands need yours.
my lips miss you.
it's not right
          if you aren't with me.

it is in the simple mornings, waking by your side, singing along with the birds.

it warms us on the cold nights when i pull you closer, snuggling deeper.

it is in the quiet days spent by your side, working on our own things together.

it is in the meals we make and in each bite as we enjoy it together.

it is love.

a kiss from you
creates warmth.
it is winter now,
and snow falls.
so kiss me.

smiling and sipping lemonade
on a summer's sunny day.
cuddling and kissing
on a cold winter's night.

don't forget to save some water to water your own soil.
it is easy to give and give, i know. you can't forget about
you, though. if you run out of water for yourself, how can
you water others? a tree can't provide much shade if all the
leaves have fallen off. a flower doesn't bloom without the
rain. why do you help everyone else grow and bloom, but
deny yourself that beauty?

let yourself bloom.

if a butterfly can cause a hurricane,
imagine what you could cause.

love isn't about proposals, regardless of how *spectacular* or *long-awaited* they are. it's not about *grand trips to faraway places* with days of expenses and nights of fancy lingerie. *it's not about couples*, even; it runs far deeper than that. love is the *mixture of people*, sometimes more mixed than others. it's in *remembering to kiss them* before you leave. it's about taking out and bringing in the garbage cans each week, *without being asked*. it's about the way a *stranger's* smile seems to always make *you* smile, too, or the way a woman sings that makes your heart feel like it is going to burst. it's about *connection*, over and over and over. you know him, he knows her, she knows them, and they know me. it's about common ideas and interests, and it can also be about respectfully disagreeing. love is not about hate; it doesn't focus on disagreements and imperfections. it's about building bridges and allowing people to cross. it's about understanding one another, even if you're not eye-to-eye. love is *allowing yourself to be weak*, although it is never weak to ask for help. it is about returning their kindness with your own. an eye for an eye, not in *punishment* but in i. it's about small gifts simply because *it made me think of you*. love isn't about materials, it's not something you can touch. it's a feeling, sometimes in your chest, or your stomach, or maybe in the warmth of a hug. it's intangible, but the feeling it brings, the happiness and light it gives to the darkest of lives, *that is love*. love is bright and warm. it changes lives. it's necessary for a happy life. it's needed in many ways: loving others, but also in needing others to love you, *including yourself*.

- *thank you*

Made in the USA
Las Vegas, NV
01 July 2024

91701362R00085